Sous Vide Made

Easy

An Amazing Guide With New Modern Technique for

Cooking your Favorite Sous Vide Dishes

Charlotte Green

Disclaimer Notice:

Please note the information contained within this document is for educational and entertainment purposes only. All effort has been executed to present accurate, up to date, and reliable, complete information. No warranties of any kind are declared or implied. Readers acknowledge that the author is not engaging in the rendering of legal, financial, medical or professional advice. The content within this book has been derived from various sources. Please consult a licensed professional before attempting any techniques outlined in this book.

By reading this document, the reader agrees that under no circumstances is the author responsible for any losses, direct or indirect, which are incurred as a result of the use of information contained within this document, including, but not limited to, errors, omissions, or inaccuracies.

Table of Content

Breakfast

Spicy Giardiniera

Preparation Time: 30 minutes, Cooking time: 1 hours,

Servings: 8

Ingredients

•   2 cups white wine vinegar

•   1 cup water

•   ½ cup beet sugar

•   3 tablespoons kosher salt

•   1 tablespoon whole black peppercorns

•   1 cup cauliflower, cut up into ½-inch pieces

•   1 stemmed and seeded bell pepper, cut up into ½-inch

pieces

•   1 cup carrots, cut up into ½-inch pieces

•   ½ thinly sliced white onion

•   2 seeded and stemmed Serrano peppers, cut up into ½-

inch pieces

Directions:

1. Prepare the Sous-vide water bath using your immersion circulator and raise the temperature to 180°F.

2. Take a large bowl and mix in vinegar, sugar, salt, water, and peppercorns.

3. Transfer the mixture to a large resealable zipper bag and add the cauliflower, onion, serrano peppers, vinegar mixture, bell pepper, and carrots.

4. Seal it up using the immersion method and submerge underwater, cook for about 1 hour.

5. Once cooked, take it out from the bag and serve

Nutrition: Calories 247, Carbohydrates 42 g, Fats 7 g, Protein 4 g

Radishes with "Vegan" Butter

Preparation Time: 5 minutes, Cooking time: 45 minutes,

Servings: 4

Ingredients

- 1-pound radishes, cut up in half lengthwise

- 3 tablespoons vegan butter

- ½ teaspoon sea salt

Directions:

1. Prepare your Sous Vide water bath using your immersion circulator and raise the temperature to 190°F.

2. Add your radish halves, butter, and salt in a resealable zipper bag and seal it up using the immersion method.

3. Submerge underwater and cook for 45 minutes.

4. Once cooked, strain the liquid and discard.

5. Serve the radishes in a bowl!

Nutrition: Calories 205, Carbohydrates 30 g, Fats 9 g, Protein 1 g

Sous-vide Rhubarb

Preparation Time: 15 minutes, Cooking time: 40 minutes,

Servings: 4

Ingredients

*   2 cups rhubarb

*   1 tablespoon Grand Marnier

*   1 teaspoon beet sugar

*   ½ teaspoon kosher salt

*   ½ a teaspoon freshly ground black pepper

Directions:

1.   Prepare the Sous-vide water bath to a temperature of 140°F using your immersion circulator.

2.   Take a large heavy-duty resealable zip bag and add all the listed ingredients. Whisk everything well.

3.   Seal the bag using the immersion method/water displacement method.

4.   Place it under your preheated water and cook for about 40 minutes.

5.   Once cooked, take the bag out from the water bath, take the contents out and place it on a serving plate.

6.   Serve warm!

Nutrition: Calories 112, Carbohydrates 27 g, Fats 0 g, Protein 1 g

Chipotle & Black Beans

Preparation Time: 25 minutes, Cooking time: 6 hours,

Servings: 6

Ingredients

- 1 cup dry black beans

- 2 2/3 cup water

- 1/3 cup freshly squeezed orange juice

- 2 tablespoons orange zest

- 1 teaspoon salt

- 1 teaspoon cumin

- ½ teaspoon chipotle chili powder

Directions:

1. Prepare the Sous-vide water bath using your immersion circulator and raise the temperature to 193°F.

2. Take a heavy-duty resealable plastic bag and add the listed ingredients into the bag.

3. Submerge it underwater and cook for 6 hours.

4. Once cooked, take the bag out from the water bath.

5. Pour the contents into a nice sauté pan and place it over medium heat.

6. Simmer until the amount has been reduced.

7. Once your desired texture is achieved, remove from the heat and serve!

Nutrition: Calories 473, Carbohydrates 15 g, Fats 37 g, Protein 20 g

Cheesy Chicken Balls

Preparation Time: 1 hour 15 minutes

Cooking Time: 25-75 minutes

Servings: 6

Ingredients:

- 1 pound ground chicken

- 2 tbsp onion, finely chopped

- ¼ tsp garlic powder

- Salt and black pepper to taste

- 2 tbsp breadcrumbs

- 1 egg

- 32 small, diced cubes of mozzarella cheese

- 1 tbsp butter

- 3 tbsp panko

- ½ cup tomato sauce

- ½ oz grated Pecorino Romano cheese

- Chopped parsley

Directions:

1. Prepare a water bath and place the Sous Vide in it. Set to 146 F. In a bowl, mix the chicken, onion, salt, garlic powder, pepper and seasoned breadcrumbs. Add the egg and combine well. Form 32 medium-size balls and fill with a cube of cheese, make sure the mix covers the cheese well.

2. Place the balls in a vacuum-sealable bag and let chill for 20 minutes. Then, release air by the water displacement method, seal and submerge the bag in the water bath. Cook for 45 minutes.

3. Once the timer has stopped, remove the balls. Heat the butter in a skillet over medium-high heat and add the panko. Cook until toast. As well cook the tomato sauce. In a servings dish, place the balls and glaze with the tomato sauce. Top with the panko and cheese. Garnish with parsley.

Nutrition: Calories 352, Fat 5, Fiber 3, Carbs 7, Protein 5

Sage Infused Turkey

Preparation Time: 10 minutes

Cooking Time: 12 hours

Servings: 4-6

Ingredients:

- 2 turkey legs and thighs, with bone and skin

- 1 lemon, sliced

- 10 sage leaves

- 4 cloves garlic, halved

- Salt, to taste

- 1 teaspoon black peppercorns

Directions:

1. Preheat Sous Vide water bath to 148F.

2. Season the turkey with salt and place in a Sous Vide bag.

3. Add the lemon slices, sage, garlic, and peppercorns.

4.   Vacuum seal the bag and cook the turkey 12 hours.

5.   Finishing steps:

6.   Remove the turkey from the bag and pat dry.

7.   Heat non-stick skillet over medium-high heat.

8.   Sear the turkey until golden-brown.

9.   Serve warm.

Nutrition: Calories 334, Fat 33, Fiber 3, Carbs 14, Protein 7

Cheesy Turkey Burgers

Preparation Time: 1 hour 45 minutes

Cooking Time: 25-75 minutes

Servings: 6

Ingredients:

- 6 tsp olive oil

- 1½ pounds ground turkey

- 16 cream crackers, crushed

- 2½ tbsp chopped fresh parsley

- 2 tbsp chopped fresh basil

- ½ tbsp Worcestershire sauce

- ½ tbsp soy sauce

- ½ tsp garlic powder

- 1 egg

- 6 buns, toasted

- 6 tomato slices

- 6 Romaine lettuce leaves

- 6 slices Monterey Jack cheese

Directions:

1. Prepare a water bath and place the Sous Vide in it. Set to 148 F. Combine the turkey, crackers, parsley, basil, soy sauce and garlic powder. Add the egg and mix using your hands.

2. In a baking sheet with wax pepper, with the mixture create 6 patties and place them. Cover it and transfer into the fridge

3. Remove the patties from the fridge and place it in three vacuum-sealable bag. Release air by the water displacement method, seal and submerge the bag in the water bath. Cook for 1 hour and 15 minutes.

4. Once the timer has stopped, remove the patties. Discard the cooking juices.

5. Heat the olive oil in a skillet over high heat and place the patties. Sear for 45 seconds per side. Place the patties over the toasted buns. Top with tomato, lettuce and cheese. Serve.

Nutrition: Calories 352, Fat 5, Fiber 3, Carbs 7, Protein 5

White Beans

Preparation Time: 15 minutes, Cooking time: 3-4 hours,

Servings: 8

Ingredients

- 1 cup dried and soaked navy beans

- 1 cup water

- ½ cup extra-virgin olive oil

- 1 peeled carrot, cut up into 1-inch dices

- 1 stalk celery, cut up into 1-inch dices

- 1 quartered shallot

- 4 cloves crushed garlic

- 2 sprigs fresh rosemary

- 2 pieces' bay leaves

- Kosher salt, to taste

- Freshly ground black pepper, to taste

Directions:

1. Prepare your Sous-vide water bath using your immersion circulator and raise the temperature to 190°F.

2.   Carefully drain and rinse your beans and add them alongside the rest of the ingredients to a heavy-duty zip bag.

3.   Seal using the immersion method and submerge it underwater. Cook for about 3 hours.

4.   Once cooked, taste the beans.

5.   If they are firm, then cook for another 1 hour and pour them in a serving bowl.

6.   Serve!

Nutrition: Calories 218, Carbohydrates 36 g, Fats 2 g, Protein 14 g

Truffle Sunchokes

Preparation Time: 15 minutes, Cooking time: 90 minutes,

Servings: 4

Ingredients

- 8 ounces peeled Sunchokes, sliced into ¼ inch thick pieces

- 3 tablespoons unsalted vegan butter

- 2 tablespoons agave nectar

- 1 teaspoon truffle oil

- Kosher salt, and black pepper, to taste

Directions:

1. Prepare the Sous Vide water bath using your immersion circulator and raise the temperature to 180°F.

2. Take a heavy-duty resealable zip bag and add the butter, nectar, sunchokes, truffle oil and mix them well.

3. Sprinkle some salt and pepper, and then seal using the immersion method.

4. Submerge it underwater and cook for 1 ½ hour.

5.   Once cooked, transfer the contents to a skillet.

6.   Put the skillet over medium-high heat and cook for 5 minutes more until the liquid has evaporated.

7.   Season with pepper and salt to adjust the flavor if needed

8.   Serve!

Nutrition: Calories 270, Carbohydrates 40 g, Fats 10 g, Protein 5 g

Mirin Teriyaki Wings

Preparation Time: 10 minutes

Cooking Time: 45 minutes

Servings: 4

Ingredients:

- 5lb. chicken wings, sliced into flats and drumettes
- Salt and freshly ground black pepper
- 1 teaspoon teriyaki sauce
- 1 tablespoon hoisin sauce
- ½ teaspoon mirin
- ¼ teaspoon minced fresh ginger
- Vegetable oil, for frying
- Wasabi for garnish

Directions:

Set the Sous Vide cooker to 140F.

1. Season chicken wings, lightly with salt and pepper.

2.   Place wings in a zip-lock bag and seal using immersion water technique.

3.   Place the bag in a water bath and set the timer to 45 minutes.

4.   Meanwhile, prepare the sauce; combine teriyaki sauce, hoisin sauce, mirin and ginger in a bowl.

5.   Finishing steps:

6.   When the timer goes off, remove the bag and take the chicken out.

7.   Pour around 2-inches of oil in large pan and heat over medium-high heat.

8.   Fry wings for 1-2 minutes and transfer to bowl with prepared sauce; toss to combine.

9.   Serve wings on a platter, with wasabi paste.

Nutrition: Calories 334, Fat 33, Fiber 3, Carbs 14, Protein 7

Pork Bacon –The Secret Canadian Recipe

Preparation Time: 7 minutes

Cooking Time: 6 hours

Servings: 4

Ingredients:

- 8 slices Canadian bacon
- 1 teaspoon vegetable oil – optional
- Salt and pepper as needed

Directions:

1. Prepare the Sous Vide water bath using your immersion circulator and raise the temperature to 145-degrees Fahrenheit.

2. Take a resealable plastic zip bag and add the bacon in the bag.

3. Seal using the immersion method.

4. Submerge it underwater and cook for 6 hours.

5. Sprinkle with salt and pepper and serve!

Nutrition: Calories 334, Fat 33, Fiber 3, Carbs 14, Protein 7

Caesar Salad Tortilla Rolls With Turkey

Preparation Time: 1 hour 40 minutes

Cooking Time: 25-75 minutes

Servings: 4

Ingredients:

- 2 garlic cloves, minced

- 2 skinless, boneless turkey breasts

- Salt and black pepper to taste

- 1 cup mayonnaise

- 2 tbsp freshly squeezed lemon juice

- 1 tsp anchovy paste

- 1 tsp Dijon mustard

- 1 tsp soy sauce

- 4 cups iceberg lettuce

- 4 tortillas

Directions:

1. Prepare a water bath and place the Sous Vide in it. Set to 152 F. Season the turkey breast with salt and pepper and put it in a vacuum-sealable bag. Release air by the water displacement method, seal and submerge the bag in the water bath. Cook for 1 hour and 30 minutes.

2. Combine the mayonnaise, garlic, lemon juice, anchovy paste, mustard, soy sauce and remaining salt and pepper. Allow to rest in the fridge. Once the timer has stopped, remove the turkey and pat dry. Slice the turkey. Mix the lettuce with the cold dressing. Pour one-quarter of the turkey mixture into each tortilla and fold. Cut by the half and serve with the dressing.

Nutrition: Calories 352, Fat 5, Fiber 3, Carbs 7, Protein 5

Sage Turkey Roulade

Preparation Time: 5 hours 15 minutes

Cooking Time: 25-75 minutes

Servings: 6

Ingredients:

- 3 tbsp olive oil

- 2 small yellow onions, diced

- 2 stalks celery, diced

- 3 tbsp ground sage

- 2 lemons' zest and juice

- 3 cups turkey stuffing mix

- 2 cups turkey or chicken stock

- 5 pounds halved turkey breast

Directions:

1.   Place a pan over medium heat, add olive oil, onion, and celery. Sauté for 2 minutes. Add the lemon juice, zest, and sage until the lemon juice reduces.

2.   In a bowl, pour the stuffing mixture and add the cooked sage mixture. Mix it with your hands. Add in the stock gently,

while mixing with your hand until ingredients hold together well and are not runny. Gently remove the turkey meat skin and lay it on a plastic wrap. Remove bones and discard.

3.   Place the turkey breast on the skin and lay a second layer of plastic wrap on the turkey breast. Flatten it to 1 - inch of thickness using a rolling pin. Remove the plastic wrap on top and spread the stuffing on the flattened turkey, leaving ½ inch space around the edges.

4.   Starting at the narrow side, roll the turkey like a pastry roll and drape the extra skin on the turkey. Secure the roll with butcher's twine. Wrap the turkey roll in the broader plastic wrap and twist the ends to secure the roll, which should form a tight cylinder.

5.   Place the roll in a vacuum-sealable bag, release air and seal the bag. Refrigerate it for 40 minutes. Make a water bath, place Sous Vide in it, and set to 155 F. Place the turkey roll in the water bath and set the timer for 4 hours.

6.   Once the timer has stopped, remove the bag and unseal it. Preheat an oven to 400 F, remove the plastic wrap from the turkey and place it on a baking dish with skin side up. Roast

for 15 minutes. Slice in rounds. Serve with a creamy sauce and

steamed low carb vegetables.

Nutrition: Calories 352, Fat 5, Fiber 3, Carbs 7, Protein 5

Bacon & Nut Stuffed Turkey Wrapped In Ham

Preparation Time: 3 hours 45 minutes

Cooking Time: 25-75 minutes

Servings: 6

Ingredients:

- 1 white onion, chopped

- 3 tbsp butter

- 1 cup bacon cubes

- 4 tbsp pine nuts

- 2 tbsp chopped thyme

- 4 garlic cloves, minced

- Zest of 2 lemons

- 4 tbsp chopped parsley

- ¾ cup bread crumbs

- 1 egg, beaten

- 4 lb boneless turkey breast, butterflied

- Salt and black pepper to taste

- 16 slices ham

Directions:

1.   Prepare a water bath and place the Sous Vide in it. Set to 146 F.

2.   Heat 2 tbsp of the butter in a skillet over medium heat and sauté the onion for 10 minutes until softened. Set aside. To the same skillet, add the bacon and cook for 5 minutes until brown. Stir in the pine nuts, thyme, garlic and lemon zest and cook for 2 minutes more. Add the parsley and mix. Return the onion to the skillet, add in bread crumbs and egg and stir well.

3.   Take out the turkey and cover it with plastic wrap. With a meat hammer pound it to the thickness. Place the ham in an aluminium foil. Put the turkey on the ham and smash the center to create a strip. Roll the turkey tightly from one side to other until is completely wrapped. Cover the wrapped turkey with plastic wrap and place it in a vacuum-sealable bag. Release air by the water displacement method, seal and submerge the bag in the water bath. Cook for 3 hours.

4.   Once the timer has stopped, remove the turkey and discard the plastic. Heat the remaining butter in a skillet over medium heat and put the breast. Sear the ham for 45 seconds per side. Roll the turkey and sear for 2-3 minutes more. Cut the breast into medallions and serve.

Nutrition: Calories 352, Fat 5, Fiber 3, Carbs 7, Protein 5

Bacon Strips & Eggs

Preparation Time: 10 minutes

Cooking Time: 60 minutes

Servings: 2

Ingredients:

- 4 egg yolks

- 2 slices British-style bacon rashers cut up into ½ inch by 3-inch slices

- 4 slices crisp toasted bread

Directions:

1. Prepare the Sous Vide water bath using your immersion circulator and raise the temperature to 143-degrees Fahrenheit.

2. Gently place each of your egg yolks in the resealable zipper bag and seal it using the immersion method.

3. Submerge it underwater and cook for about 1 hour.

4. In the meantime, fry your bacon slices until they are crisp.

5. Drain them on a kitchen towel.

6.   Once the eggs are cooked, serve by carefully removing the yolks from the zip bag and placing it on top of the toast.

7.   Top with the slices of bacon and serve!

Nutrition: Calories 334, Fat 33, Fiber 3, Carbs 14, Protein 7

Thyme Turkey Breast

Preparation Time: 3 hours 15 minutes

Cooking Time: 25-75 minutes

Servings: 6

Ingredients:

- 1 turkey breast half, boneless with skin on

- 1 tbsp olive oil

- 1 tbsp garlic salt

- 1 tbsp thyme

- 1 tsp black pepper

Directions:

1. Prepare a water bath and place the Sous Vide in it. Set to 146 F.

2. Combine the turkey breast, garlic, thyme, salt and pepper. Place it in a vacuum-sealable bag. Release air by the water displacement method, seal and submerge the bag in the water bath. Cook for 4 hours.

3.	Once the timer has stopped, remove the bag and pat dry with a baking sheet. Heat an iron skillet over high heat and sear for 5 minutes until golden.

Nutrition: Calories 352, Fat 5, Fiber 3, Carbs 7, Protein 5

Duck Confit

Preparation Time: 15 minutes + inactive time

Cooking Time: 12 hours

Servings: 2

Ingredients:

- 2 duck legs, skin on, bone in

- 3 sprigs marjoram

- 1 tablespoon green peppercorns

- 1 tablespoon fine salt

- ½ cup duck Fat

- 2 fresh bay leaves

Directions:

1. Rub the duck with marjoram, peppercorns, and salt.

2. Place in a clean vessel and refrigerate 24 hours.

3. Preheat Sous Vide cooker to 170F.

4. Remove the duck from a vessel, rinse, and pat dry. Place the duck into Sous Vide bag, along with duck Fat, and bay leaves.

5. Vacuum seal and cook 12 hours in a water bath.

6. Finishing steps:

7. When the timer goes off, remove the duck.

8. Heat the nonstick skillet and cook the duck, skin side down, 5 minutes.

9. Serve.

Nutrition: Calories 334, Fat 33, Fiber 3, Carbs 14, Protein 7

Pork Cheeks

Preparation Time: 30 minutes

Cooking Time: 5 hours

Servings: 4

Ingredients:

- 1 lb. skinless pork cheeks
- Kosher salt, and black pepper, as needed
- 1 cup beef stock
- ½ cup tomato sauce
- 1 stalk celery, cut up into 1-inch dice
- 1 quartered shallot
- 3 sprigs fresh thyme
- 1 oz. whiskey
- Mashed potatoes

Directions:

1.   Prepare the Sous Vide water bath using your immersion circulator and increase the temperature to 180-degrees Fahrenheit.

2. Take the cheeks and season it with salt and pepper and transfer them to a heavy-duty resealable zip bag.

3. Add in the stock, tomato sauce, shallot, whiskey, celery, and thyme to the bag.

4. Seal up the bag using the immersion method and submerge it underwater. Cook for 5 hours.

5. Once cooked, remove the bag and transfer it to a plate.

6. Strain the cooking liquid through a fine mesh strainer into a large saucepan. Discard any solid remains.

7. Bring the mixture to a simmer by placing it over medium-high heat.

8. Reduce the heat to medium-low and keep simmering for 20 minutes.

9. Lower down the heat to low levels and transfer the cheeks.

10. Simmer for 2-3 minutes.

11. Serve with the mashed potatoes.

Nutrition: Calories 334, Fat 33, Fiber 3, Carbs 14, Protein 7

Lunch

Pork

Preparation Time: 5 minutes, Cooking time: 3 hours 10 minutes, Servings: 4

Ingredients:

- 1-pound pork tenderloin
- 2 garlic cloves, coarsely chopped
- 2 tbsp garlic powder
- 2 tbsp ground paprika
- Salt and pepper to taste
- 1 tbsp dried oregano
- ½ tsp liquid smoke
- ¼ cup BBQ sauce

Directions:

1. Preheat the water bath to 150°F.

2. Mix salt, pepper, garlic powder, paprika and oregano in a bowl.

3.   Rub the pork with the spice mixture and put it into the vacuum bag.

4.   Add 1 garlic clove to the bag.

5.   Seal the bag and cook in the preheated water bath for 3 hours.

6.   When the time is up, carefully removing the pork from the bag and sear it on both sides over the high heat in 1 tbsp olive oil until light brown.

7.   Slice the pork and serve with the BBQ sauce.

Nutrition: Calories 246, Carbohydrates 11 g, Fats 14 g, Protein 19 g

Cocktails And Infusions

Infused Blackberry Syrup

Preparation Time: 10 minutes, Cooking time: 2 hours,

Servings: 8

Ingredients:

- 1.5lb. blackberries

- 4 cups water

- 4 cups sugar

- 4 sprigs basil

Directions:

1. Preheat Sous vide to 135°F.

2. In a Sous Vide bag combine all ingredients.

3. Seal the bag and submerge in a water bath.

4. Cook 2 hours.

5. Remove the bag from the cooker.

6. Place the bag in an ice-cold water and cool 30 minutes.

7. Strain the infusion into a glass jar.

8. Serve or store in a fridge.

Nutrition: Calories 441.2, Carbohydrates 108.2 g, Fats 0.4 g,

Protein 1.2 g

Sherry Braised Pork Ribs

Preparation Time: 10 minutes, Cooking time: 18 hours 10 minutes, Servings: 4

Ingredients:

- 2 pounds pork ribs, chopped into bone sections
- 1 tbsp ginger root, sliced
- ½ tsp ground nutmeg
- 2 tbsp soy sauce
- 1 tsp salt
- 1 tsp white sugar
- 1 anise star pod
- ¼ cup dry sherry
- 1 tbsp butter

Directions:

1.   In a small bowl, combine salt, sugar and ground nutmeg, and rub the pork ribs with this mixture.

2.   Put the ribs into the vacuum bag, add sliced ginger root, soy sauce, anise star and sherry wine.

3.   Preheat your sous vide machine to 176°F.

4.   Set the cooking time for 18 hours.

5.   When the time is up, carefully dry the ribs with the paper towels.

6.   Sear the ribs in 1 tbsp butter on both sides for about 40 seconds until crusty.

Nutrition: Calories 284, Carbohydrates 32 g, Fats 12 g, Protein 12 g

Chili Pork Chops

Preparation Time: 5 minutes, Cooking time: 1 hour 10 minutes, Servings: 2

Ingredients:

- 2 pork rib chops
- 1 small onion, chopped
- 2 garlic cloves
- 2 tbsp Worcestershire sauce
- ½ tsp chili powder
- Salt and pepper to taste
- 1 tbsp unsalted butter
- 1 tbsp vegetable oil

Directions:

1. In a small bowl, mix salt, pepper and chili powder.
2. Rub the pork chops and put them into the vacuum bag.
3. Preheat your sous vide machine to 144°F.

4.   Add the garlic cloves, chopped onion, Worcestershire sauce and olive oil to the bag and seal it.

5.   Set the cooking time for 1 hour.

6.   When the time is up, carefully dry the chops with the paper towels.

7.   Sear the chops in 1 tbsp butter on both sides for about 40 seconds (until light brown).

Nutrition: Calories 289, Carbohydrates 15 g, Fats 13 g, Protein 28 g

Grand Marnier

Preparation Time: 5 minutes, Cooking time: 1 hour 30 minutes, Servings: 12

Ingredients

- Zest, 8 large orange
- 2 cups brandy
- ½ cup ultrafine sugar

Directions:

1. Prepare your Sous Vide water bath using your immersion circulator and raise the temperature to 180°F.

2. Add all the listed ingredients to a resealable zip bag.

3. Seal using the immersion method.

4. Cook for 90 minutes.

5. Strain and discard the orange zest.

6. Allow it to chill and serve when needed!

Nutrition: Calories 190, Carbohydrates 39 g, Fats 2 g, Protein 4 g

Dinner

Chicken and Red Beans

Preparation time: 10 minutes

Cooking time: 1 hour

Servings: 4

Ingredients:

- 1 pound chicken breasts, skinless, boneless and cubed

- 1 tablespoon olive oil

- 1 cup canned red kidney beans, drained and rinsed

- ½ cup tomato sauce

- 1 red onion, sliced

- 1 tablespoon chives, chopped

- ½ teaspoon chili powder

Directions:

1. In a large sous vide bag, mix the chicken with the oil, beans and the other ingredients, seal the bag and cook in the water bath at 175 degrees F for 1 hour.

2. Divide the mix between plates and serve.

Nutrition: calories 231 fat 12 fiber 4 carbs 7 protein 15

Chicken with Brussels Sprouts Mix

Preparation time: 10 minutes

Cooking time: 50 minutes

Servings: 4

Ingredients:

- 1 pound chicken breast, skinless, boneless and cubed

- 2 tablespoons olive oil

- 2 cups Brussels sprouts, trimmed and halved

- 2 tablespoons lime juice

- 2 tablespoons lime zest, grated

- ½ teaspoon chili powder

- 3 garlic cloves, minced

- A pinch of salt and black pepper

- 1 tablespoon parsley, chopped

Directions:

1. In a large sous vide bag, mix the chicken with the oil, sprouts and the other ingredients, toss, seal the bag, submerge in the water oven, cook at 175 degrees F for 50 minutes, divide the mix between plates and serve.

Nutrition: calories 253 fat 14 fiber 2 carbs 7 protein 16

Turkey and Fennel

Preparation time: 10 minutes

Cooking time: 1 hour

Servings: 4

Ingredients:

• 2 pounds turkey breast, skinless, boneless and roughly cubed

• 1 tablespoon olive oil

• 2 fennel bulbs, sliced

• Juice of 1 lime

• 1 teaspoon sweet paprika

• 1 tablespoon rosemary, chopped

• A pinch of salt and black pepper

• 1 tablespoon dill, chopped

Directions:

1. In a sous vide bag, mix the turkey with the oil, fennel and the other ingredients, seal the bag, cook in the water oven at 175 degrees F for 1 hour, divide the mix between plates and serve.

Nutrition: calories 273 fat 13 fiber 3 carbs 7 protein 17

Rosemary Chicken

Preparation time: 10 minutes

Cooking time: 1 hour

Servings: 4

Ingredients:

- 2 pounds chicken breast, skinless, boneless and cubed
- 2 tablespoons olive oil
- Juice of 1 lime
- 1 tablespoon rosemary, chopped
- 2 garlic cloves, minced
- 1 teaspoon chili powder

Directions:

1. In a large sous vide bag, mix the chicken with the oil and the other ingredients, seal the bag and cook in the water bath at 175 degrees F for 1 hour.

2. Divide everything between plates and serve.

Nutrition: calories 263 fat 12 fiber 5 carbs 7 protein 16

Cumin Turkey

Preparation time: 10 minutes

Cooking time: 50 minutes

Servings: 4

Ingredients:

- 1 red onion, sliced

- 2 pounds turkey breast, skinless, boneless and sliced

- Juice of ½ lemon

- 2 tablespoons olive oil

- 2 garlic cloves, minced

- 1 tablespoon cumin, ground

- A pinch of salt and black pepper

- 2 tablespoons chives, chopped

Directions:

1.   In a large sous vide bag, mix the turkey with the onion, lemon juice and the other ingredients, seal the bag and cook in the water bath at 180 degrees F for 50 minutes.

2.   Divide everything between plates and serve with a side salad.

Nutrition: calories 214 fat 14 fiber 2 carbs 6 protein 15

Chicken with Endives

Preparation time: 10 minutes

Cooking time: 1 hour

Servings: 4

Ingredients:

- Zest of 1 lime, grated

- ½ teaspoon coriander, ground

- ½ teaspoon cumin, ground

- ½ teaspoon basil, dried

- ½ tablespoon olive oil

- 1 tablespoon chives, chopped

- 1 pound chicken breast, skinless, boneless and sliced

- 2 endives, shredded

- 1 red onion, sliced

- ½ cup white wine

Directions:

1.   In a large sous vide bag, mix the chicken with the endives, onion and the other ingredients, toss, seal the bag,

submerge in the water oven and cook at 180 degrees F for 1 hour.

2.	Divide the mix between plates and serve.

Nutrition: calories 276 fat 15 fiber 3 carbs 7 protein 16

Cinnamon Chicken

Preparation Time: 10 minutes

Cooking Time: 1 hour

Servings: 4

Ingredients:

- 2 pounds chicken breasts, skinless, boneless and sliced

- 1 tablespoon cinnamon powder

- 2 tablespoons lemon juice

- ¼ cup chicken stock

- 2 tablespoons avocado oil

- 3 scallions, chopped

- A pinch of salt and black pepper

- 1 teaspoon chili powder

- 2 tablespoons cilantro, chopped

Directions:

1.   In a sous vide bag, mix the chicken with the cinnamon, lemon juice, stock and the other ingredients, toss, seal the bag and cook in the water oven at 170 degrees F for 1 hour.

2.   Divide the mix between plates and serve.

Nutrition: Calories 364, Fat 23.2, Fiber 2.3, Carbs 5.1, Protein 35.4

Balsamic Turkey

Preparation time: 10 minutes

Cooking time: 1 hour

Servings: 4

Ingredients:

- 1 pound turkey breast, skinless, boneless and sliced

- 2 tablespoons olive oil

- 2 tablespoons balsamic vinegar

- 2 garlic cloves, minced

- A pinch of salt and black pepper

- 1 tablespoon chives, chopped

Directions:

1. In a sous vide bag, mix the turkey with the oil, vinegar and the other ingredients, seal the bag and cook in the water bath at 174 degrees F for 1 hour.

2. Divide the mix between plates and serve with a side salad.

Nutrition: calories 252 fat 15 fiber 2 carbs 6 protein 15

Allspice Turkey

Preparation Time: 10 minutes

Cooking Time: 50 minutes

Servings: 4

Ingredients:

- 2 pounds turkey breasts, skinless, boneless and cubed

- 1 red onion, chopped

- ½ teaspoon rosemary, dried

- ¼ cup red wine

- 2 tablespoons avocado oil

- 1 teaspoon allspice, ground

- 1 tablespoon chives, chopped

Directions:

1. In a large sous vide bag, combine the turkey with the onion, allspice and the other ingredients, seal the bag, cook in the water oven at 180 degrees F for 50 minutes, divide the mix between plates and serve.

Nutrition: Calories 238, Fat 9.7, Fiber 1, Carbs 2.9, Protein 33.3

Oregano Turkey

Preparation Time: 10 minutes

Cooking Time: 50 minutes

Servings: 4

Ingredients:

- 2 pounds turkey breast, skinless, boneless and cubed

- 2 tablespoons avocado oil

- 3 garlic cloves, minced

- 2 tablespoons oregano, chopped

- ½ cup white wine

- A pinch of salt and black pepper

- 1 teaspoon rosemary, dried

Directions:

1. In a sous vide bag, mix the turkey with the oil, oregano and the other ingredients, seal the bag, submerge in the water oven and cook at 170 degrees F for 50 minutes.

2. Divide the mix between plates and serve.

Nutrition: Calories 183, Fat 2.5, Fiber 1.2, Carbs 1.5, Protein 13.4

Chicken with Okra

Preparation Time: 10 minutes

Cooking Time: 1 hour

Servings: 4

Ingredients:

- 2 pounds chicken breast, skinless, boneless and cubed

- 1 red onion, chopped

- 1 cup okra, sliced

- 2 tablespoons olive oil

- 2 tablespoons lime juice

- 1 tablespoon balsamic vinegar

- A pinch of salt and black pepper

- ½ teaspoon turmeric powder

- 1 tablespoon oregano, chopped

Directions:

1. In a large sous vide bag, mix the chicken with the onion, okra and the other ingredients, seal the bag, submerge in the water bath and cook at 180 degrees F for 1 hour.

2. Divide everything between plates and serve.

Nutrition: Calories 256, Fat 12.6, Fiber 0.6, Carbs 1.2, Protein

33.2

Snack

Panko Yolk Croquettes

Preparation Time: 60 minutes

Servings: 5

Ingredients:

- 2 eggs plus 5 yolks

- 1 cup panko breadcrumbs

- 3 tbsp olive oil

- 5 tbsp flour

- ¼ tsp italian seasoning

- ½ tsp salt

- ¼ tsp paprika

Directions:

1.   Prepare a water bath and place the Sous Vide in it. Set to 150 F. Place the yolk inside the water (without a bag or glass and cook for 45 minutes, turning over halfway through. Let cool slightly. Beat the eggs along with the other ingredients, except the oil. Dip the yolks in the egg and panko mixture.

2.   Heat the oil in a skillet. Fry the yolks for a few minutes per side, until golden.

Nutrition: calories 170, fat 2, fiber 1, carbs 6, protein 6

Cherry Chicken Bites

Preparation Time: 1 hour and 40 minutes

Servings: 3

Ingredients:

- 1 pound chicken breast, boneless and skinless, cut into bite-sized pieces
- 1 cup red bell pepper, chopped into chunks
- 1 cup green bell pepper, chopped into chunks
- 1 cup cherry tomatoes, whole
- 1 cup olive oil
- 1 tsp Italian seasoning mix
- 1 tsp cayenne pepper
- ½ tsp dried oregano
- Salt and black pepper to taste

Directions:

1.   Rinse the meat under cold running water and pat dry with a kitchen paper. Cut into bite-sized pieces and set aside. Wash the bell peppers and cut them into chunks. Wash the cherry tomatoes and remove the green stems. Set aside.

2.   In a bowl, combine olive oil with Italian seasoning, cayenne, salt, and pepper.

3.   Stir until well incorporated. Add the meat and coat well with the marinade. Set aside for 30 minutes to allow flavors to meld and penetrate into the meat.

4.   Place the meat along with vegetables in a large vacuum-sealable bag. Add three tablespoons of the marinade and seal the bag. Cook en sous vide for 1 hour at 149 F.

Nutrition: calories 180, fat 11, fiber 2, carbs 8, protein 13

Chicken Fingers

Preparation Time: 2 hours 20 minutes

Servings: 3

Ingredients:

- 1 pound chicken breast, boneless and skinless

- 1 cup almond flour

- 1 tsp minced garlic

- 1 tsp salt

- ½ tsp cayenne pepper

- 2 tsps mixed Italian herbs

- ¼ tsp black pepper

- 2 eggs, beaten

- ¼ cup olive oil

Directions:

1. Rinse the meat under cold running water and pat dry with a kitchen paper. Season with mixed Italian herbs and place in a large vacuum-sealable. Seal the bag and cook en sous vide for 2 hours at 167 F. Remove from the water bath and set aside.

2. Now combine together flour, salt, cayenne, Italian herbs, and pepper in a bowl and set aside. In a separate bowl, beat the eggs and set aside.

3. Heat up olive oil in a large skillet, over medium heat. Dip the chicken into the beaten egg and coat with the flour mixture. Fry for 5 minutes on each side, or until golden brown.

Nutrition: calories 204, fat 15, fiber 2, carbs 3, protein 4

Lemon & Garlick Artichokes

Preparation Time: 2 hours 15 minutes

Servings: 5

Ingredients:

• 3 Artichokes

• Juice from 3 Lemons

• 1 tbsp Mustard

• 5 Garlic Cloves, minced

• 1 tbsp minced Green Onion

• 4 tbsp Olive Oil

Directions:

1. Prepare a water bath and place the Sous Vide in it. Set to 195 F. Wash and separate the artichokes. Place in a plastic bowl. Add the remaining ingredients and shake to coat well. Place all the mixture in a plastic bag. Seal and submerge the bag in water bath.Set the timer for 2 hours.

2. Once the timer has stopped, remove the bag and cook on the grill for a minute per side.

Nutrition: Calories: 109 Total Fat – 10.1g Total Carb: 5.6g

Dietary Fiber: 1.9g Protein: 4.8g

Cauliflower Bowls

Preparation time: 10 minutes

Cooking time: 50 minutes

Servings: 8

Ingredients:

- 2 eggs, whisked
- 2 cups cauliflower florets
- 1/3 cup parmesan, grated
- 1/3 cup breadcrumbs
- 2 tablespoons chives, chopped
- Cooking spray
- Salt and black pepper to the taste

Directions:

1. In a sous vide bag, combine the cauliflower with salt and pepper, grease with cooking spray, toss, seal the bag, submerge it in your preheated water oven and cook at 183 degrees F for 40 minutes.

2. In a bowl, mix the cauliflower with the rest of the ingredients, toss well, transfer the bites to another sous vide

bag, seal, submerge them in the water oven and cook them at 180 degrees F for 10 minutes.

3.   Divide into bowls and serve as a snack.

Nutrition: calories 140, fat 4, fiber 2, carbs 7, protein 7

Cinnamon Persimmon Toast

Preparation Time: 4 hours 10 minutes

Servings: 6

Ingredients:

- 4 Bread Slices, toasted

- 4 Persimmons, chopped

- 3 tbsp Sugar

- ½ tsp Cinnamon

- 2 tbsp Orange Juice

- ½ tsp Vanilla Extract

Directions:

1.   Prepare a water bath and place the Sous Vide in it. Set to 155 F.

2.   Place persimmons in a vacuum-sealable bag. Add in orange juice, vanilla extract, sugar, and cinnamon. Close the bag and shake well to coat the persimmon pieces. Release air by the water displacement method, seal and submerge the bag in water bath.Set the timer for 4 hours.

3.   Once the timer has stopped, remove the bag and transfer the persimmons to a food processor. Blend until smooth. Spread the persimmon mixture over the toasted bread.

Nutrition: calories 180, fat 11, fiber 2, carbs 8, protein 13

Parmesan Chicken Wings

Preparation time: 10 minutes

Cooking time: 4 hours

Servings: 6

Ingredients:

- 2 pounds chicken wings, halved

- 2 tablespoons olive oil

- 1 tablespoon soy sauce

- 1 tablespoon sugar

- Salt and black pepper to the taste

- ½ teaspoon Italian seasoning

- ½ cup parmesan cheese, grated

Directions:

1. In a sous vide bag, combine the chicken wings with the oil and the other ingredients except the parmesan, toss, seal the bag, submerge them in the preheated water oven and cook at 170 degrees F for 4 hours.

2. Arrange the chicken wings on a platter, sprinkle the parmesan on top and serve as an appetizer.

Nutrition: calories 154, fat 8, fiber 1, carbs 6, protein 14

Spicy Meatballs

Preparation time: 10 minutes

Cooking time: 1 hour

Servings: 12

Ingredients:

- 2 eggs, whisked

- 1 pound beef stew meat, ground

- 1 tablespoon garlic, minced

- ½ teaspoon chili powder

- ½ teaspoon hot paprika

- 4 spring onions, chopped

- Salt and black pepper to the taste

- ¼ cup almond flour

- ½ teaspoon garlic powder

- 2 tablespoon basil, chopped

Directions:

1.   In a bowl, combine the meat with the eggs and the other ingredients, stir well and shape medium meatballs out of this mix.

2. Divide them into sous vide bags and keep them in the freezer for 10 minutes.

3. Submerge sous vide bags in the preheated water oven and cook at 145 degrees F for 1 hour.

4. Arrange the meatballs on a platter and serve.

Nutrition: calories 130, fat 6, fiber 3, carbs 5, protein 7

Dessert

Vegetable Frittata

Preparation Time: 35 minutes, Cooking time: 1 hour, Servings:

5

Ingredients

- 1 tablespoon extra-virgin olive oil

- 1 medium onion, chopped

- Kosher salt

- 4 cloves garlic, minced

- 1 small rutabaga, peeled, diced

- 2 medium-sized carrots, peeled, diced

- 1 medium-sized parsnip, peeled, diced

- 1 cup butternut squash, peeled, diced

- 6 oz. oyster mushrooms, roughly chopped, trimmed

- ¼ cup fresh parsley leaves, minced

- A pinch of red pepper flakes

- 5 large whole eggs

- ¼ cup whole milk

Directions:

1.   Prepare your Sous Vide water bath using your immersion circulator and raise the temperature to 176°F

2.   Grease your canning jars with oil

3.   Take a large-sized skillet and add the oil in it and place over a medium high heat

4.   Add your onions to the heated skillet, stir cook for about 5 minutes, season with some salt

5.   Add the garlic and stir cook for few more minutes

6.   Add the carrots, rutabaga, mushrooms, butternut squash and parsnips, season with some salt and cook for 10-15 more minutes

7.   Stir in the pepper flakes and parsley

8.   Take a large liquid measuring cup and whisk in eggs and milk, season the mix with salt

9.   Divide the egg mixture amongst the jars together with the vegetables

10.   Wipe off the tops, using a damp cloth, and tighten the lids using the fingertip method

11.   Place the jars in your water bath and cook them for 60 minutes

12.   Once done, remove the jars from your water bath and remove the lids

13.   Allow to cool and serve!

Nutrition: Calories 459, Carbohydrates 34 g, Fats 23 g, Protein 29 g

Apple & Cauliflower Soup

Preparation Time: 30 minutes, Cooking time: 1 hour, Servings: 8

Ingredients

- 2 tablespoons extra-virgin olive oil

- 1 large onion, diced

- 2 garlic cloves, thinly sliced

- Kosher salt as needed

- ⅛ teaspoon crushed red chili flakes

- 1 large cauliflower head, chopped into medium florets

- 1 apple, peeled and diced

- 4-6 cups vegetable broth

Directions:

1.   Prepare the Sous Vide water bath using your immersion circulator and increase the temperature to 183°F

2.   Place a medium-sized skillet over a medium heat, add the oil and allow the oil to shimmer

3.   Add the onion, ¼ teaspoon of salt, and garlic and sauté for 7 minutes until they are tender

4.   Add the chili flakes and stir well

5.   Once done, turn-off the heat and allow the mixture to cool

6.   Divide the apple, the onion mix, cauliflower, and ¼ teaspoon of salt between two individual resealable bags

7.   Seal the bags using the immersion method, submerge and cook for 1 hour

8.   Once done, remove the bag and place the contents in a large pot

9.   Add the vegetable broth and blend well using an immersion blender

10.   Add a bit more broth for a thicker consistency

11.   Season with salt and serve

Nutrition: Calories 207, Carbohydrates 19 g, Fats 11 g, Protein 8 g

Blueberry Jam

Preparation Time: 10 minutes, Cooking time: 1 hour 30 minutes, Servings: 10

Ingredients:

- 2 cups blueberries
- 1 cup white sugar
- 2 tbsp lemon juice

Directions:

1. Preheat the water bath to 180°F.

2. Put the ingredients into the vacuum bag and seal it.

3. Cook for 1 hour 30 minutes in the water bath.

4. Serve over ice cream or cake, or store in the fridge in an airtight container.

Nutrition: Calories 74, Carbohydrates 13 g, Fats 2 g, Protein 1 g

Honey Glazed Purple Carrots

Preparation Time: 10 minutes, Cooking time: 45 minutes,

Servings: 4

Ingredients:

- 1lb. purple carrots, scrubbed

- ¾ cup orange juice

- 2 tablespoons acacia honey

- 2 teaspoons orange zest

- 1 sprig mint

- 1 teaspoon cumin

- Salt and pepper, to taste

Directions:

1. Preheat your sous Vide to 185°F.

2. Combine all ingredients into a Sous Vide bag.

3. Vacuum seal the bag and submerge carrots in the heated water.

4. Cook the carrots 45 minutes.

5. Remove the bag from the Sous Vide appliance.

6. Open and serve warm.

Nutrition: Calories 78.2, Carbohydrates 17.7 g, Fats 0.2 g,

Protein 1.4 g

Cauliflower and Chard Mix

Preparation time: 10 minutes

Cooking time: 1 hour

Servings: 6

Ingredients:

- 1 pound cauliflower florets

- 1 cup red chard, torn

- 1 tablespoon olive oil

- 1 tablespoon lemon juice

- 1 tablespoon balsamic vinegar

- 1 tablespoon lemon zest, grated

- ½ teaspoon garlic powder

- ½ teaspoon rosemary, dried

- Salt and black pepper to the taste

- 1 cup red onion, chopped

- 1 tablespoon chives, chopped

Directions:

1. In a sous vide bag, combine the cauliflower with the chard, oil and the other ingredients, toss, seal the bag, submerge in the preheated water oven and cook at 185 degrees F for 1 hour.

2. Divide the mix between plates and serve as a side salad.

Nutrition: calories 171 fat 20 fiber 2 carbs 3 protein 4

Ginger Broccoli and Radish Mix

Preparation time: 10 minutes

Cooking time: 40 minutes

Servings: 4

Ingredients:

- 1 pound broccoli florets
- ½ pound radish, halved
- 2 tablespoons olive oil
- 1 tablespoon soy sauce
- 2 teaspoons coriander seeds, crushed

- 1 yellow onion, chopped

- Salt and black pepper to the taste

- A pinch of red pepper, crushed

- 1 tablespoon ginger, grated

- 1 garlic clove, minced

- 1 tablespoon chives, chopped

Directions:

1.   In a sous vide bag, combine the broccoli with the radishes, oil and the other ingredients, seal the bag, submerge in the preheated water oven and cook at 183 degrees F for 40 minutes.

2.   Divide the mix between plates and serve as a side dish.

Nutrition: calories 150 fat 4 fiber 2 carbs 7 protein 12

Yogurt & Caraway Soup

Preparation Time: 25 minutes, Cooking time: 2 hours 8 minutes, Servings: 4

Ingredients

- 1 tablespoon extra-virgin olive oil
- 1½ teaspoons caraway seeds
- 1 medium onion, diced
- 1 leek, halved and thinly sliced
- Kosher salt
- 2 pounds red beets, peeled, chopped
- 1 bay leaf
- 3 cups chicken broth
- ½ cup whole milk yogurt
- Apple cider vinegar
- Fresh dill fronds

Directions:

Prepare your Sous Vide water bath using your immersion circulator and raise the temperature to 185°F

1.   Add the oil in a large skillet and heat it over medium heat

2.   When the oil is shimmering, add your caraway seeds

3.   Toast them for about 1 minute

4.   Put the onion, pinch of salt and leek, and sauté them for 5-7 minutes until the leek and onion are tender

5.   Put the bay leaf, beets, and ½ teaspoon of salt into a large bowl and mix them well

6.   Divide the mixture between two heavy-duty, resealable zipper bags and seal them using the displacement/water immersion method

7.   Submerge the bag under water for about 2 hours

8.   Once done, take the bags out and pour the contents to a large-sized bowl or pot.

9.   Add the chicken broth and blend the whole mixture using an immersion blender

10.   Stir in the yogurt, with some extra water or broth if you want a different consistency

11.   Season the soup with some salt and vinegar

12.   Serve with a garnish of dill fronds!

Nutrition: Calories 208, Carbohydrates 16 g, Fats 12 g, Protein 9 g

Peas & Shallots

Preparation Time: 5 minutes, Cooking time: 1 hour, Servings: 8

Ingredients

- 1 lb. fresh sweet peas
- 1 cup heavy cream
- ¼ cup butter
- 1 tablespoon cornstarch
- ¼ teaspoon ground nutmeg
- 4 cloves
- 2 bay leaves
- Freshly ground black pepper

Directions:

1. Prepare your water bath using your Sous Vide immersion circulator and raise the temperature to 184°F

2. Put the cornstarch, butter, nutmeg and cream into a small bowl

3. Whisk well until the cornstarch has fully dissolved

4.　　Put the mixture into a zip bag together with the peas, black pepper, cloves, bay leaves, and seal using the immersion method

5.　　Submerge underwater and cook for 1 hour

6.　　Discard the bay leaf and serve!

Nutrition: Calories 155, Carbohydrates 17 g, Fats 7 g, Protein 6 g

Miso Roasted Celeriac

Preparation Time: 30 minutes, Cooking time: 2 hours,

Servings: 6

Ingredients

- 1 tablespoon miso paste

- 1 whole celeriac

- 6 cloves garlic

- 5 sprigs thyme

- 1 teaspoon onion powder

- 3 tablespoon feta cheese

- 1 tablespoon mustard seeds

- Juice of ¼ a large lemon

- 5 cherry tomatoes roughly cut

- Chopped up parsley

- 8-ounce vegan butter

- 1 tablespoon olive oil

- 8-ounce cooked quinoa

Directions:

1. Prepare the Sous Vide water bath using your immersion circulator and raise the temperature to 185°F

2. Take a large-sized pan and place it over medium heat, add the garlic, thyme, feta cheese, and dry fry them for 1 and a ½ minute

3. Add the butter and keep stirring until slightly browned

4. Add the onion powder and keep the mixture on the side and allow it to cool at room temperature

5. Add the celeriac to a zip bag alongside the cooled butter mixture

6. Submerge and cook for 1½ to 2 hours

7. Transfer the mixture to a hot pan (place over medium heat) and stirring it until golden brown

8. Season with miso paste

9. Add the oil to another pan and place it over medium heat, add the tomatoes, mustard seeds and re-heat the quinoa

10. Carefully add the lemon and parsley to the previously made tomato mixture

11. Assemble your platter by transferring the celeriac and tomato mix

12.   Serve!

Nutrition: Calories 203, Carbohydrates 5 g, Fats 15 g, Protein 12 g

Green Beans and Walnuts Mix

Preparation time: 10 minutes

Cooking time: 1 hour

Servings: 4

Ingredients:

- 1 tablespoon balsamic vinegar

- 2 tablespoons olive oil

- Salt and black pepper to the taste

- 5 scallions, chopped

- A handful cilantro, chopped

- 1 pound green beans, trimmed

- 1 cup walnuts, chopped

- 1 tablespoon soy sauce

Directions:

1.   In a sous vide bag, combine the green beans with the walnuts, soy sauce and the other ingredients, seal the bag, submerge in your preheated water oven and cook at 185 degrees F for 1 hour.

2.   Divide the mix between plates and serve as a side dish.

Nutrition: calories 170 fat 5 fiber 3 carbs 4 protein 6

Persimmon Chutney

Preparation Time: 25 minutes, Cooking time: 1 hour 30 minutes, Servings: 4

Ingredients

- 2 lbs. fuyu persimmons, peeled, diced into small pieces
- 1 small onion, diced
- ½ cup light brown sugar
- ¼ cup raisins
- 2 tablespoons apple cider vinegar
- 2 tablespoons freshly squeezed lemon juice
- 1½ teaspoons yellow mustard seeds
- 1½ teaspoons coriander seeds
- ½ teaspoon kosher salt
- ¼ teaspoon curry powder
- ¼ teaspoon dried ginger
- ⅛ teaspoon cayenne

Directions:

1.   Prepare your Sous Vide water bath using your immersion circulator and raise the temperature to 183°F

2.   Put all the ingredients into a large, heavy-duty resealable bag

3.   Seal it using the immersion method and submerge

4.   Cook for 90 minutes

5.   Once done, remove the bag and transfer it to a storage container

6.   Serve cool

Nutrition: Calories 333, Carbohydrates 79 g, Fats 1 g, Protein 2 g

Lemon Olives and Radish Mix

Preparation time: 10 minutes

Cooking time: 30 minutes

Servings: 4

Ingredients:

- 2 tablespoons olive oil

- 2 garlic cloves, minced

- 1 tablespoon lemon juice

- 1 teaspoon sweet paprika

- 1 teaspoon lemon zest, grated

- Salt and black pepper to the taste

- 1 cup black olives, pitted

- 1 cup kalamata olives, pitted

- 1 cup radishes, halved

Directions:

1. In a sous vide bag, combine the olives with the radishes, oil and the other ingredients, seal the bag, submerge into your preheated water oven and cook at 134 degrees F for 30 minutes.

2.   Divide between plates and serve.

Nutrition: calories 130 fat 20 fiber 4 carbs 7 protein 1

Lightning Source UK Ltd.
Milton Keynes UK
UKHW021126110521
383520UK00001B/132